Ice cream & milkshakes

Ice cream & milkshakes

Delicious and cooling summertime treats

First published in 2012
LOVE FOOD is an imprint of Parragon Books Ltd

Parragon
Queen Street House
4 Queen Street
Bath BA1 1HE, UK

ISBN: 978-1-4454-6927-0

Printed in China

Designed by Sabine Vonderstein
Introduction by Linda Doeser

Notes for the Reader
This book uses standard kitchen measuring spoons and cups. All
spoon and cup measurements are level unless otherwise indicated.
Unless otherwise stated, milk is assumed to be whole, eggs are large,
individual vegetables are medium, and pepper is freshly ground black
pepper.

The times given are only an approximate guide. Preparation times differ
according to the techniques used by different people and the cooking
times may also vary from those given. Optional ingredients, variations, or
serving suggestions have not been included in the calculations. Recipes
using raw or very lightly cooked eggs should be avoided by infants, the
elderly, pregnant women, and anyone with a chronic illness. Pregnant
and breast-feeding women are advised to avoid eating peanuts and
peanut products. People with nut allergies should be aware that some
of the prepared ingredients used in the recipes in this book may contain
nuts. Always check the packaging before use.

The publisher would like to thank Corbis for permission to reproduce
the following copyright material: front cover image, Menu Illustration of
Waitress Carrying Ice Cream Desserts.

Contents

Introduction

There is no treat more delicious on a hot summer's day than ice cream, but sometimes it can be disappointing because it turns out to be more ice than cream! The best way to avoid such a let-down is to make your own—and it's easier than you think. As well as a rich and voluptuous texture, homemade ice creams are packed with real flavors, not artificial chemicals. And the range of mouthwatering flavors is huge, from classics, such as vanilla and chocolate chip, to taste sensations, such as green tea and cherry. The following pages are filled with great ideas for ice creams and sorbets that make cooling summery snacks and refreshing family and party desserts, guaranteed to delight the child in all of us. To top it off—literally—there's a choice of delicious sauces to mix and match with your favorite ice creams.

Milkshakes are also a summer favorite, especially among children. From a parent's point of view, they provide an easy way to encourage children to drink milk, so they can benefit from its rich supply of vitamins and minerals, and they are also a great way to increase their intake of fruit. From a child's point of view, they're just fun, colorful, and delicious. And when they're homemade with plenty of fresh ingredients and are so easily put together, they will taste twice as good.

Of course, milkshakes are not just a treat for children. Because they can be blended in minutes, they are a wonderful way to get the day off to a good start for teenagers—and adults, too—as well as being a healthier alternative to commercially produced high-sugar soft drinks for quenching your thirst.

You won't need any hard-to-find ingredients to make these wonderful concoctions and they won't create havoc with the family budget. However, as with any food, it's worth buying good-quality ingredients. For the best flavor, fruit should be ripe, eggs should be fresh, and chocolate should have a high percentage of cocoa solids.

A freezer and food processor or blender are essential, and that's about it! The only real advantage of an ice cream machine is that the process is quicker than doing it by hand. However, the initial cost can be expensive and you will need to find a place in the kitchen to store it.

If you already have one or feel inspired to buy one, simply follow the manufacturer's directions for freezing. Inexpensive plastic storage containers with airtight lids or even old plastic containers from store-bought ice cream are perfectly fine for storage, which, given how great these recipes are, isn't likely to be for long.

So head to the refrigerator and pantry for a few basic ingredients, add some fresh fruit, and get ready to delight your friends and family. All that's left to do is to start working your way through this gorgeous book, and add making ice cream and milkshakes to your list of culinary skills!

Cool Classics

Mascarpone Ice Cream

Serves 4

1/2 cup mascarpone cheese
2 cups heavy cream
2/3 cup whole milk
4 egg yolks
1/2 cup granulated sugar
1/2 teaspoon vanilla extract
(optional)

Beat together the mascarpone and ¼ cup of the heavy cream until thick and stiff, then chill in the refrigerator until ready to use.

Add the remaining heavy cream and the milk to a heavy saucepan, slowly bring to a simmer over low heat, then remove from the heat. Put the egg yolks and sugar in a bowl and beat together until pale and the mixture leaves a trail when the beaters are lifted. Add the hot cream mixture and beat thoroughly.

Return the cream-and-egg mixture to the rinsed-out saucepan and cook over low heat for 10–15 minutes, stirring continuously, until the mixture thickens enough to coat the back of the wooden spoon. Do not let the mixture boil or it will curdle. Remove the mixture from the heat and submerge the bottom of the pan in a bowl of ice-cold water to stop the cooking process. Let cool for at least 1 hour, stirring occasionally to prevent a skin from forming. When the cream-and-egg mixture is cool, beat in the chilled mascarpone mixture and the vanilla extract, if using.

If using an ice cream machine, churn the mixture following the manufacturer's directions. Alternatively, freeze in a freezer-proof container, uncovered, for 1–2 hours, or until it begins to set around the edges. Transfer the mixture to a bowl and stir with a fork until smooth. Return to the container and freeze for an additional 2–3 hours or until completely frozen.

To store, cover the container with a suitable lid. Remove the ice cream from the freezer and place in the refrigerator for 15–20 minutes before serving.

Chocolate Milkshake

Serves 2

2/3 cup whole milk
2 tablespoons chocolate syrup
3 cups chocolate ice cream
grated chocolate, to decorate

Pour the milk and chocolate syrup into a food processor or blender and process gently until combined.

Add the chocolate ice cream and process until smooth. Pour the mixture into glasses and decorate with the chocolate.

Serve immediately.

Chocolate Chip Ice Cream

Serves 4–6

1¼ cups milk

1 vanilla bean

3 egg yolks

½ cup granulated sugar

1¼ cups whipping cream

4 ounces milk chocolate, chopped into small pieces

chocolate-coated ice cream cones, to serve

Pour the milk into a heavy saucepan, add the vanilla bean, and place over low heat. Slowly bring to a simmer and remove from the heat. Let steep for 30 minutes. Put the egg yolks and sugar in a bowl and beat together until pale and the mixture leaves a trail when the beaters are lifted. Remove the vanilla bean from the milk, then add the milk to the sugar mixture and beat thoroughly.

Return the mixture to the rinsed-out saucepan and cook over low heat for an additional 10–15 minutes, stirring all the time, until the mixture thickens enough to coat the back of the wooden spoon. Do not let the mixture boil or it will curdle.

Remove the mixture from the heat and submerge the bottom of the pan in a bowl of ice-cold water to stop the cooking process. Let cool for at least 1 hour, stirring occasionally to prevent a skin from forming. Meanwhile, whip the cream until it holds its shape. Keep in the refrigerator until ready to use.

If using an ice cream machine, fold the whipped cream into the mixture, then churn the mixture following the manufacturer's directions. Just before the ice cream freezes, add the chocolate pieces. Alternatively, fold the whipped cream into the mixture and freeze in a freezer-proof container, uncovered, for 1–2 hours, or until it begins to set around the edges. Transfer the mixture to a bowl and stir with a fork until smooth. Add the chocolate pieces. Return to the container and freeze for an additional 2–3 hours or until completely frozen. To store, cover the container with a suitable lid. Remove the ice cream from the freezer and place in the refrigerator for 15–20 minutes before serving. Scoop the ice cream into cones to serve.

Strawberries & Cream Milkshake

Serves 2

1 cup frozen strawberries
1/2 cup light cream
1 cup cold whole milk
1 tablespoon granulated sugar
mint leaves, to decorate

Put the strawberries, cream, milk, and sugar into a food processor or blender and process gently until combined.

Pour the mixture into glasses and decorate with the mint leaves.

Serve immediately.

Toffee Ice Cream

Serves 6

1¼ cups whole milk

3 egg yolks

⅓ cup firmly packed light brown sugar

16-ounce jar Dulce de Leche (caramel sauce)

1¼ cups whipping cream

Pour the milk into a heavy saucepan, slowly bring to a simmer over low heat, then remove from the heat. Put the egg yolks and sugar in a bowl and beat together until pale and the mixture leaves a trail when the beaters are lifted. Add the milk and beat thoroughly.

Return the mixture to the rinsed-out saucepan and cook over low heat for an additional 10–15 minutes, stirring all the time, until the mixture thickens enough to coat the back of the wooden spoon. Do not let the mixture boil or it will curdle.

Remove the mixture from the heat, add the caramel sauce, and beat together until smooth. Submerge the bottom of the pan in a bowl of ice-cold water to stop the cooking process. Let cool for at least 1 hour, stirring occasionally to prevent a skin from forming. Meanwhile, whip the cream until it holds its shape. Keep in the refrigerator until ready to use.

If using an ice cream machine, fold the whipped cream into the mixture, then churn the mixture following the manufacturer's directions. Alternatively, fold the whipped cream into the mixture and freeze in a freezer-proof container, uncovered, for 1–2 hours, or until it begins to set around the edges. Transfer the mixture to a bowl and stir with a fork until smooth. Return to the container and freeze for an additional 2–3 hours, or until completely frozen.

To store, cover the container with a suitable lid. Remove the ice cream from the freezer and place in the refrigerator for 15–20 minutes before serving.

Mocha Cream

Serves 2

1 cup milk

1/4 cup light cream

1 tablespoon brown sugar

2 tablespoons unsweetened cocoa powder

1 tablespoon coffee syrup or instant coffee powder

6 ice cubes

whipped cream and grated chocolate, to decorate

Put the milk, cream, and sugar into a food processor or blender and process gently until combined.

Add the cocoa powder and coffee syrup and process well, then add the ice cubes and process until smooth.

Pour the mixture into glasses and decorate with the cream and chocolate.

Serve immediately.

Chocolate Fudge Ice Cream

Serves 4–6

1¹/4 cups milk

4 ounces semisweet dark chocolate, broken into pieces

2 tablespoons butter

1 teaspoon vanilla extract

¹/2 cup granulated sugar

¹/3 cup light corn syrup

4 eggs

1¹/4 cups whipping cream

wafer sticks, to serve

Pour ¾ cup of the milk into a heavy saucepan. Add the chocolate, butter, and vanilla extract and heat gently over low heat, stirring continuously. Stir in the sugar and syrup and heat until the mixture boils. Reduce the heat and simmer for 4 minutes, without stirring. Remove from the heat.

Put the eggs in a bowl and beat together. Add the chocolate mixture, stirring continuously.

Return the mixture to the rinsed-out saucepan and cook over low heat for an additional 10–15 minutes, stirring continuously, until the mixture thickens enough to coat the back of the wooden spoon. Do not let the mixture boil or it will curdle.

Remove the mixture from the heat, add the remaining milk, and the cream and stir together until smooth. Submerge the bottom of the pan in a bowl of ice-cold water to stop the cooking process. Let cool for at least 1 hour, stirring occasionally to prevent a skin from forming.

If using an ice cream machine, churn the mixture following the manufacturer's directions. Alternatively, freeze in a freezer-proof container, uncovered, for 1–2 hours, or until it begins to set around the edges. Transfer the mixture to a bowl and stir with a fork until smooth. Return to the container and freeze for an additional 2–3 hours, or until completely frozen.

To store, cover the container with a suitable lid. Remove the ice-cream from the freezer and place in the refrigerator for 15–20 minutes before serving. Serve with wafer sticks.

Italian Vanilla Gelato

Serves 6–8

1³/₄ cups milk
1 vanilla bean
6 egg yolks
²/₃ cup granulated sugar
ice cream cones, to serve

Pour the milk into a heavy saucepan. Split open the vanilla bean and scrape out the seeds into the milk, then add the whole vanilla bean. Place over low heat, slowly bring to a simmer, then remove from the heat. Let steep for 30 minutes. Put the egg yolks and sugar in a bowl and beat together until pale and the mixture leaves a trail when the beaters are lifted. Remove the vanilla bean from the milk, then add the milk to the sugar mixture and beat thoroughly.

Return the mixture to the rinsed-out saucepan and cook over low heat for an additional 10–15 minutes, stirring all the time, until the mixture thickens enough to coat the back of the wooden spoon. Do not let the mixture boil or it will curdle.

Remove the mixture from the heat and submerge the bottom of the pan in a bowl of ice-cold water to stop the cooking process. Let cool for at least 1 hour, stirring occasionally to prevent a skin from forming.

If using an ice cream machine, churn the mixture following the manufacturer's directions. Alternatively, freeze in a freezer-proof container, uncovered, for 1–2 hours, or until it begins to set around the edges. Transfer the mixture to a bowl and stir with a fork until smooth. Return to the container and freeze for an additional 2–3 hours, or until completely frozen.

To store, cover the container with a suitable lid. Remove the ice cream from the freezer and place in the refrigerator for 15–20 minutes before serving. Scoop the ice cream into cones to serve.

Rum & Raisin Ice Cream

Serves 6

1/2 cup raisins

3 tablespoons rum

2 1/2 cups whipping cream

1 vanilla bean

4 extra-large egg yolks

1/2 cup granulated sugar

Put the raisins in a bowl, add the rum, and stir together. Let soak for 2–3 hours, stirring occasionally, until the liquid is absorbed. Meanwhile, pour the cream into a heavy saucepan. Split open the vanilla bean and scrape out the seeds into the cream, then add the whole vanilla bean. Place over low heat, slowly bring to a simmer, then remove from the heat. Let steep for 30 minutes. Put the egg yolks and sugar in a bowl and beat together until pale and the mixture leaves a trail when the beaters are lifted. Remove the vanilla bean from the cream, then add the cream to the sugar mixture and beat thoroughly.

Return the mixture to the rinsed-out saucepan and cook over low heat for an additional 10–15 minutes, stirring continously, until the mixture thickens enough to coat the back of the wooden spoon. Do not let the mixture boil or it will curdle.

Remove the mixture from the heat and submerge the bottom of the pan in a bowl of ice-cold water to stop the cooking process. Let cool for at least 1 hour, stirring occasionally to prevent a skin from forming.

If using an ice cream machine, churn the mixture following the manufacturer's directions. Just before the ice cream freezes, add the soaked raisins. Alternatively, freeze in a freezer-proof container, uncovered, for 1–2 hours, or until it begins to set around the edges. Transfer the mixture to a bowl and stir with a fork until smooth. Add the soaked raisins. Return to the container and freeze for an additional 2–3 hours, or until completely frozen.

To store, cover the container with a suitable lid. Remove the ice cream from the freezer and place in the refrigerator for 15–20 minutes before serving.

Fruit Flavors

Raspberry Ripple Ice Cream

Serves 6–8

1¼ cups milk
1 vanilla bean
1 cup granulated sugar
3 egg yolks
1 pint fresh raspberries
1/3 cup water
1¼ cups whipping cream

Pour the milk into a heavy saucepan, add the vanilla bean, and put over low heat. Slowly bring to a simmer and remove from the heat. Let steep for 30 minutes. Put ½ cup of the sugar and the egg yolks in a bowl and beat together until pale and the mixture leaves a trail when the beaters are lifted. Remove the vanilla bean from the milk, then add the milk to the sugar mixture and beat thoroughly. Return the mixture to the rinsed-out saucepan and cook over low heat for an additional 10–15 minutes. Do not let the mixture boil or it will curdle. Remove the mixture from the heat and submerge the bottom of the pan in a bowl of ice-cold water, to stop the cooking process. Let cool for at least 1 hour, stirring from to time to prevent a skin from forming.

Meanwhile, put the raspberries in a heavy saucepan with the remaining sugar and the water. Heat gently, until the sugar has dissolved and the raspberries are soft. Pass the raspberries through a nylon strainer into a bowl to remove the seeds, then let cool. Whip the cream until it holds its shape. Keep in the refrigerator until ready to use. If using an ice cream machine, fold the whipped cream into the mixture, then churn the mixture following the manufacturer's directions. Just before the ice cream freezes, spread half into a freezer-proof container. Pour over half of the raspberry puree, then repeat the layers. Return to the freezer for 1–2 hours, or until frozen. Alternatively, fold the whipped cream into the mixture and freeze in a freezer-proof container, uncovered, for 1–2 hours, or until it begins to set around the edges. Transfer the mixture to a bowl and stir with a fork until smooth. Spread half of the mixture into another container. Pour over half of the raspberry puree, then repeat the layers. Return to the container and freeze for an additional 2–3 hours or until completely frozen. To store, cover the container with a suitable lid. Remove the ice cream from the freezer and place in the refrigerator for 15–20 minutes before serving.

Red Berry Sorbet

Serves 6

1³/4 cups fresh red currants, plus extra to decorate, or 1³/4 cups fresh raspberries

1³/4 cups fresh raspberries, plus extra to decorate

³/4 cup water

¹/2 cup granulated sugar

²/3 cup cranberry juice

2 egg whites

wafer baskets, to serve

Strip the red currants from their stems, using the prongs of a fork, and put them in a heavy saucepan with the raspberries. Add 2 tablespoons of the water and heat gently for 5 minutes, or until the raspberries are soft. Pass the fruit through a nylon strainer into a bowl to remove the seeds, then let cool.

Put the sugar and the remaining water in the rinsed-out saucepan and heat gently, stirring, until the sugar has dissolved. Bring to a boil, then boil, without stirring, for 10 minutes to form a syrup. Do not let it brown. Remove from the heat and let cool for at least 1 hour. When cold, stir the fruit puree and cranberry juice into the syrup.

If using an ice cream machine, churn the mixture following the manufacturer's directions. When the mixture begins to freeze, beat the egg whites until stiff but not dry, then add to the mixture and continue churning. Alternatively, freeze in a freezer-proof container, uncovered, for 3–4 hours, or until mushy. Transfer the mixture to a bowl and stir with a fork until smooth. Lightly beat the egg whites until stiff but not dry, then fold them into the mixture. Return to the container and freeze for an additional 3–4 hours, or until firm.

To store, cover the container with a suitable lid. Remove the sorbet from the freezer and place in the refrigerator for 15–20 minutes before serving. Serve in wafer baskets and decorate with extra fruit.

Crushed Cherry Ice Cream

Serves 6

1/2 cup granulated sugar

2/3 cup water

12/3 cups fresh cherries, pitted, plus extra whole cherries to decorate

2 tablespoons freshly squeezed orange juice

11/4 cups heavy cream

2/3 cup light cream

Put the sugar and water in a heavy saucepan and heat gently, stirring, until the sugar has dissolved. Bring to a boil, then boil for 3 minutes. Reduce the heat, add the cherries, and simmer gently for about 10 minutes, or until soft. Let cool.

When the cherries are cold, put them into a food processor or blender with the syrup. Add the orange juice and process the cherries until just coarsely chopped. Do not blend too much—the cherries should be crushed, not pureed. Pour the heavy cream and light cream into a bowl and whip together until the mixture holds its shape. Fold in the crushed cherries.

If using an ice cream machine, churn the mixture following the manufacturer's directions. Alternatively, freeze in a freezer-proof container, uncovered, for 1–2 hours, or until it begins to set around the edges. Transfer the mixture to a bowl and stir with a fork until smooth. Return to the container and freeze for an additional 2–3 hours, or until completely frozen.

To store, cover the container with a suitable lid. Remove the ice cream from the freezer and place in the refrigerator for 15–20 minutes before serving. Serve decorated with the whole cherries.

Peach & Orange Milkshake

Serves 2

1/2 cup milk

1/2 cup peach yogurt

1/2 cup orange juice

2 cups drained canned peach slices

6 ice cubes

strips of orange peel, to decorate

Pour the milk, yogurt, and orange juice into a food processor or blender and process gently until combined.

Add the peach slices and ice cubes and process until smooth. Pour the mixture into glasses and decorate with the orange peel.

Serve immediately.

Mixed Berry Slush

Serves 2

1/4 cup orange juice

1 tablespoon lime juice

1/2 cup sparkling water

3 cups frozen mixed berries, such as blueberries, raspberries, blackberries, and strawberries

4 ice cubes

Pour the orange juice, lime juice, and sparkling water into a food processor or blender and process gently until combined.

Add the mixed berries and ice cubes, process until a slushy consistency has been reached, and pour into glasses.

Serve immediately.

Black Grape Fizz

Serves 2

1 cup black grapes,
seeded or seedless

1 cup sparkling mineral water

2 large scoops of lemon sorbet

slices of lime, to decorate

Put the grapes, mineral water, and lemon sorbet into a food processor or blender and process until smooth.

Pour into glasses and decorate with slices of lime.

Serve immediately.

Spiced Banana Milkshake

Serves 2

1¼ cups milk

½ teaspoon ground allspice, plus extra to decorate

1 cup banana ice cream

2 bananas, frozen and sliced

Pour the milk into a food processor or blender and add the allspice. Add half of the banana ice cream and process gently until combined, then add the remaining ice cream and process until well blended.

When the mixture is well combined, add the bananas and process until smooth.

Pour the mixture into glasses and decorate with a pinch of allspice.

Serve immediately.

Mango Sorbet

Serves 4–6

2 large, ripe mangoes, peeled, pitted, and chopped, juice reserved, plus extra slices to decorate

juice of 1 lemon

pinch of salt

1/2 cup granulated sugar

3 tablespoons water

Put the mango flesh into a food processor or blender. Add the mango juice, lemon juice, and salt and process until smooth. Pass the mango puree through a nylon strainer into a bowl.

Put the sugar and water in a heavy saucepan and heat gently, stirring, until the sugar has dissolved. Bring to a boil, then boil, without stirring, for 10 minutes to form a syrup. Do not let it brown. Remove from the heat and let cool slightly. Stir the mango puree into the syrup. Chill the mango syrup in the refrigerator for 2 hours, or until cold.

If using an ice cream machine, churn the mixture following the manufacturer's directions. Alternatively, freeze in a freezer-proof container, uncovered, for 3–4 hours, or until mushy. Transfer the mixture to a bowl and stir with a fork until smooth. Return to the container and freeze for an additional 3–4 hours, or until firm.

To store, cover the container with a suitable lid. Remove the sorbet from the freezer and place in the refrigerator for 15–20 minutes before serving. Serve decorated with the mango slices.

Plum Fluff

Serves 2

4 medium, ripe plums, pitted
1 cup ice-cold milk
2 scoops of vanilla ice cream

Put the plums, milk, and ice cream into a food processor or blender and process until smooth and frothy. Pour into glasses.

Serve immediately.

Something Sensational

Butterscotch & Pecan Ice Cream

Serves 6

1¼ cups milk

¼ stick butter

⅓ cup firmly packed dark brown sugar

2 eggs

⅓ cup granulated sugar

1 teaspoon vanilla extract

1¼ cups whipping cream

1 cup finely chopped pecans

Pour the milk into a heavy saucepan and bring almost to a boil. Remove from the heat. Melt the butter in a heavy saucepan, stir in the brown sugar, and heat gently until the sugar melts, then boil for 1 minute, or until beginning to caramelize, being careful not to let the mixture burn. Remove from the heat and slowly stir in the milk. Return to the heat and heat gently, stirring continuously, until well blended. Remove from the heat and let cool slightly. Put the eggs and granulated sugar in a bowl and beat together until pale. Slowly add the warm milk and vanilla extract, stirring all the time with a wooden spoon. Strain the mixture into the rinsed-out saucepan and cook over low heat for 10–15 minutes, stirring all the time, until the mixture thickens enough to coat the back of the wooden spoon. Do not let the mixture boil or it will curdle.

Remove the mixture from the heat and submerge the bottom of the pan in a bowl of ice-cold water to stop the cooking process. Let cool for at least 1 hour, stirring occasionally to prevent a skin from forming. Meanwhile, whip the cream until it holds its shape. Keep in the refrigerator until ready to use. If using an ice cream machine, fold the whipped cream into the mixture, then churn the mixture following the manufacturer's directions. Just before the ice cream freezes, add the pecans. Alternatively, fold the whipped cream into the mixture and freeze in a freezer-proof container, uncovered, for 1–2 hours, or until it begins to set around the edges. Turn the mixture into a bowl and stir with a fork until smooth. Add the pecans. Return to the container and freeze for an additional 2–3 hours, or until completely frozen. To store, cover the container with a suitable lid. Remove the ice cream from the freezer and place in the refrigerator for 15–20 minutes before serving.

Cool Minty Chocolate

Serves 4

2¹/₂ cups ice-cold milk

¹/₃ cup hot cocoa mix

1 cup light cream

1 teaspoon peppermint extract

chocolate-and-mint ice cream and fresh mint sprigs, to garnish

Pour half of the milk into a heavy saucepan and stir in the hot cocoa mix. Heat gently, stirring continuously, until just below boiling point and the mixture is smooth. Remove the saucepan from the heat.

Pour the chocolate-flavored milk into a large chilled bowl and beat in the remaining milk. Beat in the cream and peppermint extract and continue to beat until cold.

Pour the mixture into glasses, top each with a scoop of the chocolate-and-mint ice cream, and decorate with the mint sprigs.

Serve immediately.

Champagne Sorbet

Serves 6

1 cup granulated sugar

1¹/4 cups water

¹/2 bottle pink or white champagne or sparkling wine

juice of ¹/2 lemon

1 egg white

Put the sugar and water in a heavy saucepan and heat gently, stirring, until the sugar has dissolved. Bring to a boil, then boil, without stirring, for 10 minutes to form a syrup. Do not let it brown. Remove from the heat and let cool for at least 1 hour. When cold, stir the champagne and lemon juice into the syrup.

If using an ice cream machine, churn the mixture following the manufacturer's directions. When the mixture begins to freeze, beat the egg white until stiff but not dry, then add to the mixture and continue churning. Alternatively, freeze in a freezer-proof container, uncovered, for 3–4 hours, or until mushy. Transfer the mixture to a bowl and stir with a fork until smooth. Lightly beat the egg white until stiff but not dry, then fold into the mixture. Return to the container and freeze for an additional 3–4 hours, or until firm.

To store, cover the container with a suitable lid. Remove the sorbet from the freezer and place in the refrigerator for 15–20 minutes before serving.

Chocolate Praline Ice Cream

Serves 4–6

4 ounces semisweet dark chocolate, broken into pieces

1¼ cups milk

3 egg yolks

⅓ cup granulated sugar

1¼ cups whipping cream, whipped until it holds its shape

praline

vegetable oil, for brushing

½ cup granulated sugar

2 tablespoons water

⅓ cup blanched almonds

To prepare the praline, brush a baking sheet with oil. Put the sugar, water, and nuts in a heavy saucepan and heat gently, stirring, until the sugar has dissolved. Let the mixture bubble gently without stirring for 6–10 minutes. As soon as the mixture has turned golden brown, immediately pour it onto the baking sheet and spread it out evenly. Let cool for 1 hour, or until cold and hard. Finely crush the praline in a food processor. Put the chocolate and milk into a heavy saucepan and place over low heat, stirring until the chocolate is melted and the mixture is smooth. Remove from the heat. Put the egg yolks and sugar in a bowl and beat together until pale and the mixture leaves a trail when the beaters are lifted. Add the milk mixture, stirring all the time with a wooden spoon. Remove the mixture from the heat. Submerge the bottom of the pan in a bowl of ice-cold water to stop the cooking process. Let cool for at least 1 hour, stirring occasionally to prevent a skin from forming.

Return the mixture to the rinsed-out saucepan and cook over low heat for an additional 10–15 minutes, stirring all the time, until the mixture thickens enough to coat the back of the wooden spoon. Do not let the mixture boil or it will curdle. If using an ice cream machine, fold the whipped cream into the mixture, then churn the mixture following the manufacturer's directions. Just before the ice cream freezes, add the praline. Alternatively, fold the whipped cream into the mixture and freeze in a freezer-proof container, uncovered, for 1–2 hours, or until it begins to set around the edges. Transfer the mixture to a bowl and stir with a fork until smooth. Add the praline. Return to the container and freeze for an additional 2–3 hours, or until completely frozen. To store, cover the container with a suitable lid. Remove the ice cream from the freezer and place in the refrigerator for 15–20 minutes before serving.

Coffee Banana Cooler

Serves 2

1¼ cups milk
¼ cup instant coffee powder
1 cup vanilla ice cream
2 bananas, frozen and sliced

Pour the milk into a food processor or blender, add the instant coffee powder, and process gently until combined. Add half of the vanilla ice cream and process gently, then add the remaining ice cream and process until well combined.

Add the bananas and process until smooth. Pour into glasses.

Serve immediately.

Green Tea
Ice Cream

Serves 4

1 cup whole milk

2 egg yolks

2 tablespoons granulated sugar

2 tablespoons green tea powder

1/3 cup hot water

1 cup whipping cream, whipped until it holds its shape

Pour the milk into a heavy saucepan and bring almost to a boil. Remove from the heat. Put the egg yolks and sugar in a bowl and beat together until pale and the mixture leaves a trail when the beaters are lifted. Add the milk, stirring continuously with a wooden spoon.

Return the mixture to the rinsed-out saucepan and cook over low heat for an additional 10–15 minutes, stirring continuously, until the mixture thickens enough to coat the back of the wooden spoon. Do not let the mixture boil or it will curdle.

Remove the mixture from the heat and submerge the bottom of the pan in a bowl of ice-cold water to stop the cooking process. Let cool for at least 1 hour, stirring occasionally to prevent a skin from forming. Meanwhile, mix the green tea powder with the hot water and pour into the cooled mixture.

If using an ice cream machine, fold the whipped cream into the mixture, then churn the mixture following the manufacturer's directions. Alternatively, fold the whipped cream into the mixture and freeze in a freezer-proof container, uncovered, for 1–2 hours, or until it begins to set around the edges. Transfer the mixture to a bowl and stir with a fork until smooth. Return to the container and freeze for an additional 2–3 hours or until completely frozen.

To store, cover the container with a suitable lid. Remove the ice cream from the freezer and place in the refrigerator for 15–20 minutes before serving.

Pistachio Gelato

Serves 6–8

3 1/2 cups milk

1 vanilla bean

9 egg yolks

1 cup granulated sugar

2 tablespoons almond-flavored liqueur (optional)

few drops of green food coloring (optional)

3/4 cup shelled pistachio nuts, finely chopped

Pour the milk into a heavy saucepan, add the vanilla bean, and place over low heat. Slowly bring to a simmer and remove from the heat. Let steep for 30 minutes. Put the egg yolks and sugar in a bowl and beat together until pale and the mixture leaves a trail when the beaters are lifted. Remove the vanilla bean from the milk, then add the milk to the sugar mixture and beat thoroughly.

Return the mixture to the rinsed-out saucepan and cook over low heat for an additional 10–15 minutes, stirring all the time, until the mixture thickens enough to coat the back of the wooden spoon. Do not let the mixture boil or it will curdle.

Remove the mixture from the heat and submerge the bottom of the pan in a bowl of ice-cold water to stop the cooking process. Let cool for at least 1 hour, stirring occasionally to prevent a skin from forming. When cold, stir in the liqueur, if using, and the food coloring, if using.

If using an ice cream machine, churn the mixture following the manufacturer's directions. Just before the ice cream freezes, add the chopped nuts. Alternatively, freeze in a freezer-proof container, uncovered, for 1–2 hours, or until it begins to set around the edges. Transfer the mixture to a bowl and stir with a fork until smooth. Add the chopped nuts. Return to the container and freeze for an additional 2–3 hours or until completely frozen.

To store, cover the container with a suitable lid. Remove the ice cream from the freezer and place in the refrigerator for 15–20 minutes before serving.

Honeycomb Ice Cream

Serves 6–8

melted butter, for brushing
1/2 cup granulated sugar
2 tablespoons light corn syrup
1 teaspoon baking soda
1 3/4 cups whipping cream
14-ounce can condensed milk

To prepare the honeycomb, or sponge candy, brush a baking sheet with the butter. Put the sugar and corn syrup in a heavy saucepan and heat gently, stirring, until the sugar has dissolved. Boil for 1–2 minutes, or until beginning to caramelize, being careful not to let the mixture burn. Stir in the baking soda and immediately pour the mixture onto the baking sheet but do not spread. Let cool for about 10 minutes, or until cold and hard. When set, put it in a strong plastic food bag and crush into small pieces using a rolling pin.

Whip the cream until it holds its shape, then beat in the condensed milk. If using an ice cream machine, churn the mixture following the manufacturer's directions. Just before the ice cream freezes, add the crushed honeycomb, reserving a little for decoration. Alternatively, freeze in a freezer-proof container, uncovered, for 1–2 hours, or until it begins to set around the edges. Transfer the mixture to a bowl and stir with a fork until smooth. Add the crushed honeycomb, reserving a little for decoration. Return to the container and freeze for an additional 2–3 hours, or until completely frozen.

To store, cover the container with a suitable lid. Remove the ice cream from the freezer and place in the refrigerator for 15–20 minutes before serving. Serve with the reserved honeycomb.

Rocky Road Ice Cream

Serves 6–8

1¹/4 cups milk

4 ounces milk chocolate, broken into pieces

3 egg yolks

¹/2 cup granulated sugar

1¹/4 cups whipping cream

4 ounces semisweet dark chocolate, coarsely chopped

¹/3 cup blanched almonds, coarsely chopped

1 cup white miniature marshmallows, halved

¹/4 cup candied cherries, quartered

Put the milk and chocolate into a heavy saucepan and put over low heat, stirring until the chocolate is melted and the mixture is smooth. Remove from the heat. Put the egg yolks and sugar in a bowl and beat together until pale and the mixture leaves a trail when the beaters are lifted. Add the milk mixture, stirring continuously with a wooden spoon.

Return the mixture to the rinsed-out saucepan and cook over a low heat for an additional 10–15 minutes, stirring continuously, until the mixture thickens enough to coat the back of the wooden spoon. Do not let the mixture boil or it will curdle.

Remove the mixture from the heat. Submerge the bottom of the pan in a bowl of ice-cold water to stop the cooking process. Let cool for at least 1 hour, stirring occasionally to prevent a skin from forming. Meanwhile, whip the cream until it holds its shape. Keep in the refrigerator until ready to use.

If using an ice cream machine, fold the whipped cream into the mixture, then churn the mixture following the manufacturer's directions. Just before the ice cream freezes, add the chopped dark chocolate, almonds, marshmallows, and cherries. Alternatively, fold the whipped cream into the mixture and freeze in a freezer-proof container, uncovered, for 1–2 hours, or until it begins to set around the edges. Transfer the mixture to a bowl and stir with a fork until smooth. Add the chopped dark chocolate, almonds, marshmallows, and cherries. Return to the container and freeze for an additional 2–3 hours, or until completely frozen.

To store, cover the container with a suitable lid. Remove the ice cream from the freezer and place in the refrigerator for 15–20 minutes before serving.

Perfect Partners

Chocolate Sauce

Serves 4–6

1¼ cups milk

2 tablespoons butter

½ cup granulated sugar

⅓ cup firmly packed light brown sugar

1 cup unsweetened cocoa powder

ice cream, to serve

Put all the ingredients, except the ice cream, in a heavy saucepan. Heat gently, stirring all the time, until the sugar has dissolved, then bring to a boil and boil, without stirring, for 2 minutes, or until the sauce coats the back of the wooden spoon.

Serve hot or cold over ice cream.

Hot Chocolate Fudge Sauce

Serves 4–6

2 ounces semisweet dark chocolate, broken into pieces

2 tablespoons butter

1/4 cup milk

1 cup firmly packed light brown sugar

2 tablespoons light corn syrup

ice cream, to serve

This sauce should be served hot, so prepare it just before you are ready to serve the ice cream. Set a heatproof bowl over a saucepan of simmering water and add the chocolate, butter, and milk. Heat gently, stirring occasionally, until the chocolate has melted and the sauce is smooth.

Transfer the mixture to a heavy saucepan and stir in the sugar and syrup. Heat gently, stirring all the time, until the sugar has dissolved, then bring to a boil and boil, without stirring, for 5 minutes. Serve hot over ice cream.

Raspberry Sauce

Serves 6

1 pint fresh raspberries or
one 10-ounce package frozen
raspberries, thawed at room
temperature for 3–4 hours

1 teaspoon lemon juice

2 tablespoons confectioners' sugar

2 tablespoons raspberry liqueur
(optional)

ice cream, to serve

Put the raspberries and lemon juice into a food processor or blender and process to form a smooth puree. Pass the fruit through a nylon strainer into a bowl to remove the seeds.

Sift the sugar into the raspberry puree and stir together. Stir in the liqueur, if using. Chill in the refrigerator for at least 1 hour before serving. Serve cold over ice cream.

Butterscotch Sauce

Serves 6

1/4 stick butter

2/3 cup firmly packed light brown sugar

2/3 cup light corn syrup

2/3 cup heavy cream

ice cream, to serve

Put the butter, sugar, and syrup in a heavy saucepan. Heat gently, stirring continuously, until the butter has melted and the sugar has dissolved. Simmer gently, stirring occasionally, for about 5 minutes, or until a thick sauce has formed.

Remove the sauce from the heat and gradually stir in the cream. Serve hot or cold over ice cream.

Cranberry & Orange Sauce

Serves 4–6

2¹⁄3 cups fresh or frozen cranberries

1¹⁄4 cups fresh orange juice

1 cinnamon stick

¹⁄2 cup granulated sugar

juice of ¹⁄2 lemon

ice cream and wafer sticks, to serve

Put the cranberries, orange juice, and cinnamon stick in a heavy saucepan. Bring to a boil, then reduce the heat and simmer, uncovered, for 15–20 minutes, or until the cranberries have burst. Let cool slightly, then remove the cinnamon stick.

Pour the cranberries into a food processor or blender and process to form a smooth puree. Pass the fruit through a nylon strainer into a bowl to remove the seeds.

Return the cranberries to the rinsed-out saucepan and add the sugar. Heat gently, stirring all the time, until the sugar has dissolved. Stir in the lemon juice. Let the sauce cool, then chill in the refrigerator for at least 3 hours. Serve cold over ice cream, with wafer sticks.